A Day With A
MIMBRES

CONTENTS

INTRODUCTION

The ancestors of Native Americans, also called American Indians, inhabited North America before Europeans arrived in the 1500s. North America ranges from tropical (hot and lush) to arctic (cold and snowy) in climate. Bounded by oceans to the east and west, the continent is crossed by wild rivers and lined with jutting mountain ranges. Plains stretch across North America, and huge lakes dot its surface. Deserts and woodlands spread over many regions.

Early Native American cultures adapted to the environments in which they lived. In coastal regions, Native Americans hunted sea creatures and collected shellfish from the ocean waters. Inland river and lake Indians netted or speared freshwater fish in creeks, lakes, and rivers. On the wide, grassy plains, Native Americans hunted buffalo by throwing spears, by shooting arrows, or by luring the animals over cliffs. In the forests, some folks hunted deer and small mammals. In other parts of the continent, farmers grew corn, beans, and squash in small plots or large fields. Houses and clothing varied, too.

Native American belief systems also reflected environments. Some religions revolved around animals and successful hunting, the weather, the changing seasons, or the ocean. Many belief systems were **animist,** which gave every object a spirit.

Over centuries, Native Americans traveled from one end of the continent to the other and sometimes back again. These movements are remembered in the oral histories of many Indian nations and can be traced in the groups of languages that people speak. Ancient American Indians spoke more than 200 distinct languages, with thousands of dialects.

Some North American civilizations grew into huge empires ruled by powerful leaders. Large populations flooded cities that were later deserted. Small towns and villages flourished, as did nomadic communities. No one was rich or poor in some cultures, but in others some members lived in splendor while their neighbors shivered in small dwellings.

Trade routes linked people across the continent, bringing goods and new ideas from faraway places. The idea of pottery traveled from modern-day Mexico to what would later become the southwestern United States. Other people may have traded buffalo hides or meat for farm produce.

Ancient Puebloans (a people of the **Southwest** who are the ancestors of the modern Pueblo) developed different cultures in response to the world around them. This story—set in about A.D. 1130—tells about the Mimbres people who lived near the Mimbres River.

Series Editors

A DAY WITH A
MIMBRES

by J. J. Brody

Illustrations by Giorgio Bacchin

Runestone Press/Minneapolis
A Division of the Lerner Publishing Group

To Nathan, Caitlin, Thea, Ian, and Zoe

The author thanks Jean Brody, Erik Blinman, and Ed Ladd for their comments and technical advice.

All words that appear in **bold** are explained in the glossary that starts on page 43.

This edition first published in the United States in 1999 by Runestone Press.

Runestone Press, c/o The Lerner Publishing Group
241 First Avenue North, Minneapolis, MN 55401 U.S.A.

Website: www.lernerbooks.com

Photos are used courtesy of J. J. Brody, pp. 8 (left and right), 12 (top left and right), 14 (top and bottom left); Rodney Hook/Laboratory of Anthropology, Museum of New Mexico, Santa Fe, NM, p. 9 (top); Jaca Book, Milan, Italy: by M. Porta-Leva, p. 9 (bottom right), by Duilio Citi, p. 10 (middle), by Silvia Vassena, p. 11 (bottom left and right); E. Haury. *The Hohokam* (Tucson, AZ: University of Arizona Press, 1976), p. 10 (top); R. Fogt from J. J. Brody and R. Swentzell. *To Touch The Past* (New York: Hudson Hills Press, 1996), p. 13 (top and bottom). Additional artwork from Jaca Book, Milan, Italy: pp. 9 (middle), 11 (top) by G. Gaudenzi, pp. 9 (bottom left), 10 (bottom), 12 (bottom left), 14 (bottom right), 15 (images a, b, c, d, f, h) by C. Tralli, p. 12 (middle left) by M. Porta-Leva; from J. J. Brody. *Mimbres Painted Pottery* (Santa Fe, MN: The School of American Research, 1977 and 1991), p. 12 (middle right and bottom middle and right); and from O. T. Snodgrass. *Realistic Art and Times of the Mimbres Indians* (privately published, 1977), p. 15 (images e, g).

Library of Congress Cataloging-in-Publication Data

Brody, J. J.
A day with a Mimbres / by J. J. Brody ; illustrations by Giorgio Bacchin.
p. cm. — (A day with)
Includes index.
Summary: Presents both factual information and a fictional story on the customs and daily life of the Mimbres, an ancient civilization that lived in New Mexico from 200 to 1150 A.D.
ISBN 0–8225–1917–8 (lib bdg. : alk. paper)
1. Mimbres culture—Juvenile literature. 2. Indians of North America— New Mexico—Mimbres River Valley—Social life and customs— Juvenile literature. [1. Mimbres culture. 2. Indians of North America— New Mexico.] I. Bacchin, Giorgio, ill. II. Title. III. Series: Day with—
E99.M76B74   1999
305.8970—dc21   98-35121

Manufactured in the United States of America
1 2 3 4 5 6 — JR — 04 03 02 01 00 99

PART ONE

THE WORLD OF THE MIMBRES

For hundreds of years, a group of farming communities known as the Mogollon culture spread across what would become New Mexico. By the year 1130—when this story takes place—a Mogollon group known as the Mimbres had been living near the Mimbres River for at least 900 years. Like other Mogollon peoples, they built small villages—later known as **pueblos**—and farmed corn, squash, and beans.

The Mimbres lived in an area of the Southwest bounded by mountains that were too high and too cold for farming and a desert that was too arid (dry). But the mountains and desert were rich with animals and plants that the Mimbres caught, hunted, or harvested. They used parts of many plants, including the **cholla,** the **piñon,** and the **yucca.** Hunters sought bighorn sheep, deer, elk, and small animals such as rabbits and gophers. The Mimbres ate the meat, tanned the hides, and crafted the bones into tools.

The 80-mile-long Mimbres River begins in the mountains and ends in the Chihuahua Desert. The river has water in it all year. Although other rivers run through the area, many are dry for most of the year. The Mimbres lived along the 40-mile stretch of the Mimbres River Valley that was warm and wet enough for farming. Willows, cottonwood, and other trees line the green riverbanks. In fact, the word *mimbres* means "willow" in Spanish. (Centuries later, Spanish-speaking settlers from Mexico named the river after the graceful trees.)

The lush banks of the Mimbres River (below) *are located near the Galaz Ruin in New Mexico. Seen from Old Town Ruin, this view of the Mimbres Valley* (right) *is little changed since the days of the Mimbres.*

Trade linked the Mimbres to other flourishing Southwestern cultures. The Mimbres traded **cotton,** pottery, dried meat, hides, and decorative items. Westward, in what would become Arizona, the Hohokam built complex systems to irrigate (water) their desert farms and constructed massive courts for **ball games.** Northward sat Chaco Canyon, a center of trade and religion that drew travelers from across the Southwest between the years of A.D. 950 and 1150. The Mimbres also traded with southern Mimbres people of Casas Grandes in present-day Mexico.

Traders brought the Mimbres seashells from the Gulf of California, mirrors from Mexico, and scarlet macaws (large red parrots) from tropical regions farther south. Without **draft animals** or carts, people walked from region to region, carrying their goods.

Figures ring this piece of Hohokam pottery (top). A Mimbres pot from Casas Grandes, Mexico, shows its original black-and-red coloring (above). The map (left) depicts the approximate range of the pueblo cultures of the Southwest in about A.D. 1100.

Mimbres villages were made up of flat-roofed **adobe** houses with many rooms. Rooms were added as families grew. To enter and exit these dwellings, family members climbed ladders that extended through openings in roofs. Each village had a **plaza** or two, usually with a **kiva** sitting in the middle. **Ramadas** created shady areas.

Plazas, ramadas, and rooftops were where the Mimbres spent their days. Women ground corn, prepared meals, and cared for children. Women also owned the houses where people lived and were in charge of maintaining them. Kivas belonged to men, who used the spots to trade, to chat, or to perform sacred rituals. Men planted, tended, and harvested fields of corn, beans, and squash that were usually near the villages. Men also hunted and wove cotton cloth.

Between the A.D. 200 and 1150, most Mimbres villages housed less than 100 people, and the largest didn't have more than 300 inhabitants. The population was greatest from A.D. 1000 to 1150, when around 3,000 people lived in the valley. When a pueblo grew too large, a few families would found a new village nearby. The new spot and the old one kept such close ties that residents considered the two to be "sister" villages.

A long-distance traveler (top left), *with a pack and a walking staff, was redrawn from a piece of Hohokam pottery. Scarlet macaws* (middle left), *from what would become southern Mexico, were prized by the Mimbres. A masked parrot trainer is depicted on this Mimbres bowl* (bottom left).

Pueblo Bonita (inset), in northern New Mexico's Chaco Canyon, was a center of trade and religion. This reconstruction of the site shows a general outside view. At Chaco Canyon, kivas (left) were circular in shape and were usually underground. An entrance to Chaco Canyon from the south is seen from Kin Kletso (bottom left). The ancient pueblo of Chetro Ketl (below) sits in Chaco Canyon.

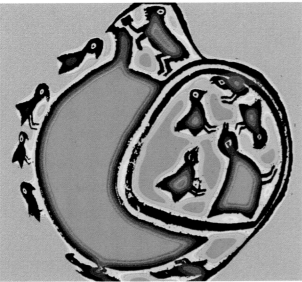

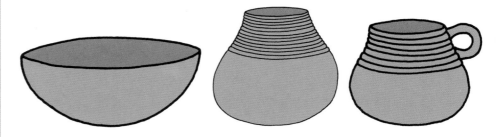

Mimbres petroglyphs (top left, top right). *A scene from Mimbres pottery* (above left) *depicting a man and birds. The Mimbres made pottery vessels* (above right) *in three shapes. They arranged their designs in three ways* (bottom right)—*a figure in the middle; figures with a blank center; and a central figure that is integrated with the framing design.*

Over time, the growing population forced people to compete for resources like firewood and meat. The climate of North America began to change, which caused longer, colder winters. The Southwest suffered from droughts and early frosts that killed crops. The deer and elk populations shrank.

Even before this climate change, Mimbres existence could be hard. Coping with the deaths of loved ones was a big part of Mimbres life. Some mourners buried human remains under the dirt floors of houses, perhaps to keep them close to the living. The Mimbres buried people with personal goods and with bowls that had been "killed" by punching a hole through the bottom.

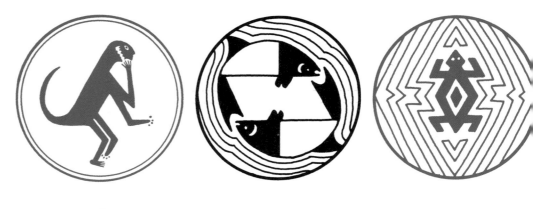

(Left) *Experts believe that the hole pierced through this bowl, which comes from a burial pit, may represent the center of the cosmos. (Below) Depicted on this Mimbres bowl from the same period is a man with a bird on his head, a walking staff, a birdcage, and a basket.*

Mimbres people ate yucca fruit and used the plant's leaves and roots. Yucca (left) flourishes in the Black Range above the Mimbres Valley. Oak and walnut trees grow nearby (below left). Imagery on pieces of pottery show that the Mimbres carried baskets (middle left) and successfully caught birds in traps (below right).

The Mimbres, like other North American Indians, didn't have a written language. People learned through their own experiences. Older members shared their wisdom with youngsters. The Mimbres respected those of great age and of wide experience.

Each Mimbres person belonged to a clan (a family group) traced through the mother. Two people from the same clan were not allowed to marry, so husbands and fathers came from different clans.

The Mimbres believed that their people had emerged from a series of underworlds and that other worlds were yet to come. Their world was centered around a mythical spot that opened to the

Some Mimbres art may depict people in rituals (top row): a) a figure that may represent death; b) a man whirling a bull-roarer (a long rope or thong with an object on the end that, when spun, makes a loud sound); c) a dancer wearing an insect costume; d) standing figures; (bottom row): e) an energetic dancer; f) a curing ceremony; g) a figure with a shield and a quiver full of arrows; and h) another dancer.

underworlds and the heights of the sky. The Mimbres believed that the world was in careful balance. Major feats—such as completing a long journey or killing a powerful animal such as a bear—upset this delicate balance. To put themselves back in harmony with the forces of the world, people underwent a **purification ritual.**

The Mimbres marked the year's progress by noting the relative position on the horizon of the sun at sunrise. They had many religious societies, one of which was probably in charge of watching the sun's movement. Also, they believed that the souls of the dead and of the not-yet-born could interact with both living people and with supernatural beings.

The Mimbres, like many other southwestern peoples, tried to control their environment with religious acts and imagery. Sufficient rainfall was the key to survival. Pottery and art at rock shrines show image after image of clouds, of lightning, and of rain falling upon the mountains.

All characters in this story are fictional. Because the Mimbres lived a long time ago and did not leave behind a written record, no one knows their real stories. But **archaeologists** and other experts know the general outlines of Mimbres lifeways.

The dry climate of the Southwest has preserved many Mimbres **artifacts,** such as buildings, pottery, and cloth. By examining these and other items, scientists learn a lot about Mimbres life. Elegant jars, bowls, and mugs show that the Mimbres had a unique style of shaping and decorating pottery. Human remains reveal to scientists how long most people lived. By studying graves, specialists have learned about how the Mimbres viewed death. Stored food shows archaeologists what the Mimbres ate, and rubbish heaps reveal what they used up or broke. Houses show building methods and the construction materials that were available. By studying shifts in the climate through time, scientists learn how the weather impacted Mimbres life. Some experts have figured out trade routes by noticing which artifacts came from far away.

Other scientists study how the modern Pueblo Native Americans remember their ancestors. Some look at traditional Pueblo life, which fills in the picture a little more. For example, Pueblo people living these days often have names that refer to nature, so maybe the ancient Mimbres did, too.

Another way to learn about the Mimbres is to figure out what challenges they faced every day. Having enough water must have worried people who lived in the dry Southwest—just as it concerns modern-day residents. The Mimbres were farmers, so they probably thought about their crops. Because the Mimbres River is lined with willow trees, the people who lived on its banks might have called it the Willow River.

The bits of information that experts gather can be carefully pieced together to create a detailed image of what Mimbres life was probably like. Let's travel to early in the morning of a day in May 1130.

PART TWO

A DAY WITH OTHERSIDE, A MIMBRES TRAVELER

In the darkness before dawn I awoke. Coyotes yipped and howled from hills rimming our river valley. It was spring but cold, so I draped a **turkey-feather blanket** over my shoulders as I rose from the sleeping mat on the hard-packed earthen floor. My wife, White Shell, was adding wood to the embers in the firepit. Our two children were asleep. I climbed the ladder to the rooftop door of our two-room apartment.

Standing on the roof, I saw the large, bright morning star hanging in the dark sky just to the south of **Horn Mountain.** The stars illuminated the jagged silhouettes of distant mountains. I softly sang a morning song as I began to twist my long hair into a club-shaped roll, called a *chongo*, at the back of my head.

The Willow River ran below the village with the last of the year's mountain snows. When spring thaws the snow of the **northern mountains** (where the river begins), the river sometimes overflows, flooding our fields. Beaver dams usually hold back most of the cold water. Except in spring and during the brief rainy time, our river is shallow and narrow. After it vanishes into the desert a couple of miles downstream, cottonwood trees grow in the dry stream bed, their long roots drinking the underground water.

I looked at the village. The shadows sharpened the edges of the homes. The plazas in front of the houses belong to the whole village, and people often work there or on the rooftops of their homes. In the plazas sit men's large kivas. On special days—when we first plant the corn or at harvesttime—that's where we have public feasts and dance ceremonies.

White Shell, her sister, her mother, and their children live in two-room or three-room apartments in this house. The women and their children are Maize Clan people, because children belong to the mother's clan. I'm Macaw Clan, and my father was Oak Clan.

Soon, when the sun rose, I would greet it—I'm in the sun-watcher religious society. The **sun priest,** White Bear, is my mother's brother, and he hopes that I'll settle down and live a good enough life to succeed him one day. But I'm not ready for that yet. I travel. About 25 years ago, when I was seven, my mother's mother got angry with me for pestering her with questions about far-off places. She chased me away, yelling: "You pesky gnat, go buzz on the other side of the mountains!" Everybody thought that was funny and began calling me Otherside. My father's sister gave me my real name, Morning Star, when I was four days old. At first, I hated being called Otherside. But now that I'm used to it, I think it's a good name. No one travels more often than I do. In fact, I'll be spending this day preparing for a journey to the stone cities of Chaco Canyon.

I heard my son, Sparrow Hawk, moving around inside the house. Just ten years old, he's my oldest, and he won't let me out of his sight. I used a strip of cotton to finish tying my chongo as the boy climbed the ladder. He was all bundled up and grinning. Sparrow Hawk looks like me—taller and leaner than most of our people, with a square face and jaw and thin lips. Sparrow Hawk would come to Chaco with me, making this his first long journey.

Sunrise was near, so Sparrow Hawk and I climbed down the outside ladder to the ground and headed for the sun-watchers shrine at the east end of the village.

Soft color tinged the eastern horizon when we joined White Bear and other members of this religious society at the sunwatchers shrine. My wife's brother Eagle Plume arrived as the first rays shot up over the top of Horn Mountain. White Bear began his chant of greeting to the sun. Sparrow Hawk quietly petted a dog while we prayed and sprinkled offerings of cornmeal to the six directions—the sky, the underworld, and the four directions on this earth surface. After the ceremony, White Bear untied a knot on a counting string, as he had each morning since midwinter's day. The knots remaining numbered the days until the **solstice.**

"Only 22 more days," he said to me. "You'll have to hurry to be at Chaco in time for the ceremonies and trade fair."

"My uncle, we leave at dawn tomorrow," I replied. "The weather should be good, and the snow is gone along our route. We'll get there in plenty of time."

Eagle Plume, who was coming with me, grinned and added: "Three years ago I raced Otherside and got there in only 15 days."

"That's right," I said, "but I still arrived first. This time, even with heavy loads and taking small steps so that Eagle Plume can keep up, I'll be there in 17 days."

It felt good to start the day with a prayer and a joke.

It was light and getting warm when we got home, so we put our warm blankets away and dressed in short-sleeved cotton shirts, cotton loincloths, and yucca-leaf sandals. Sparrow Hawk grabbed his yucca fiber bag, and we began walking down to the river to check his bird snares and my small animal traps.

A pair of black and blue Stellar jays flew noisily overhead as we scrambled down the steep slope toward the river. We stepped over the narrow irrigation ditches and crossed fields of green sprouts where, a month ago, I had worked with the other men from the village to plant clumps of corn, beans, and squash. A small cottontail rabbit and three gophers lay in the traps I had set at the edge of the fields.

We reached the willows near the river. Here Sparrow Hawk's bird snares—woven from long strands of his own hair—had caught several sparrows and a male tanager with bright yellow, black, and red feathers.

Four older women sat on the riverbank, washing their hair with frothy yucca-root suds. One, named Meadowlark, called out: "Ho, Otherside, you've been home long enough. It's time for you to be on the road! But leave Sparrow Hawk here. He's too good a hunter and too good-looking for us to let him leave!" The women laughed, but Sparrow Hawk was embarrassed.

I pretended to think deeply before replying: "Grandmother Meadowlark, I'm sorry, but my wife insists that Sparrow Hawk go with me. She's afraid you'll hurt yourselves fighting over him. Instead of Sparrow Hawk, you take these gophers and divide them among you."

Meadowlark put down her hairbrush of stiff tightly bound grass and took the animals.

"Thank you, Otherside," she said, smiling. "We'll fight over them instead of Sparrow Hawk. But you'd best be on your way or we'll take that young man, too!"

Without a word, Sparrow Hawk ran back toward the village. I followed slowly.

When we got home, everyone seemed to be outside enjoying the clear day. White Shell was kneeling at the hearth under her ramada to make **piki** on a smooth black stone. My daughter Fawn ran to greet us and to see what we had caught. Fawn is a cheerful, chubby little girl who looks like her smiling mother.

White Shell's ramada, like most on the plaza, had strips of sun-dried deer, elk, and pronghorn antelope meat on the roof, with three dressed deerskins and an elk skin dangling from the edge. All were from animals that I had killed over the winter. Although I'm not a great hunter, I'm a strong runner who can chase deer until they fall from exhaustion. Then I thank them for their sacrifice and snuff out their breath by closing their nostrils. Eagle Plume is a real hunter. He even killed a bear, an animal with so much power that he had to be purified afterwards. His mother painted a picture in a bowl that shows him shooting arrows at the bear with its cubs behind it.

As she watched the piki cook, White Shell told me that she would bundle up the meat and hides. The day before, we had made two bundles of hides and bird skins, and had filled two baskets with dried meat. I would trade the goods in Chaco Canyon. Sparrow Hawk had packed the bird skins that he had prepared himself. The northerners value the feathered skins of the small green parrots and of the other colorful birds that live in our valley.

Breakfast was ready, so we sat down in the shade under the ramada. The grayish blue piki bread was stacked high in a pottery bowl, ready to roll up and dip into cornmeal and piñon nut gruel. I told of my plans for the rest of the day, and White Shell told me her plans for the next few weeks. She and Fawn would visit the desert with a group of women to gather plants to eat and to make into medicine. White Shell told me that they would camp at the shallow lake where waterfowl come in the winter and where the cattails and bulrushes that we use to make baskets grow. But first White Shell, her mother, and her sister would prepare clay to make pottery bowls and jars to replace those that had been broken or buried in graves last winter.

Sadly, only months before, our infant son died. We buried him under the floor of White Shell's house with two of her most beautifully painted bowls. She placed other bowls in the graves of two of her sister's young children, who died only a short time after our son. The children's spirits will take the bowls, each with a hole punched in the bottom, on their journeys to the beautiful underworld where they will join our ancestors. When they can, they'll help those of us who remain on the surface of this earth.

Long ago, Mother Earth took clay from her own body and used it to form people. Later she gave women the gift of making pottery in which to cook, store, and serve food. The beautiful pottery reminds us of lost loved ones and great deeds. Many pieces of pottery are painted with pictures of clouds, of rain, and of the harmony of the universe. Others show great deeds. Men sometimes paint pictures on pottery, but only women make it.

We never bring much food on trips. It's easier to hunt animals and to gather wild plants on the way. After breakfast, Sparrow Hawk followed me to the edge of the village where we make arrowheads. Eagle Plume was there already, expertly hammering a stone against a chisel made from an elk's antler. The chisel rested on a chunk of black obsidian, a volcanic glass that traders had brought from mountains northwest of us. With each blow, Eagle Plume chiseled off large flakes of the obsidian. Sparrow Hawk and I would shape these flakes into arrowheads sharp enough to pierce the toughest hides.

My son and I set to work, chipping off tiny fragments of the obsidian. The razor-like chips can fly in any direction, so we work in an out-of-the-way place. Careful though we are, we always nick ourselves. Sparrow Hawk is learning to chip stone by watching and practicing. He gripped a flake of obsidian in his left palm, which was protected by a piece of buckskin, and then he chipped the edge of the obsidian with an antler tip held in his right hand. He worked the flakes into inch-long triangles that I chipped into sharp arrowheads.

When we had finished 10 arrowheads, Eagle Plume wrapped them and the chunks of obsidian in separate pieces of buckskin. He would add these to the others we had already made. I put my bundles and my tools into a soft leather pouch that I hung over my shoulder with a strap. The pouch also held fire-making tools and necessities like cornmeal.

Eagle Plume decided to go to our kiva, where he and the others who were coming to Chaco would finish packing for the long journey. But Sparrow Hawk and I set off toward the next village downstream, our sister village, to meet with some traders from the south.

I hoped that they would have valuable scarlet macaws, seashells, and copper bells. I had tied a bag of turquoise and shell jewelry at my waist to exchange for those southern goods. Storyteller, my Macaw Clan brother from the sister village, would introduce me to the traders. Then, he would spend the night at my village and walk to Chaco Canyon with us to trade his cotton wool. Sparrow Hawk and I slung our canteens over our shoulders, I took my walking staff, and we trotted off.

The sun was high when my son and I left the village and walked down the grassy natural **terrace** to cross the river south of the farms. **Turkey vultures** drifted in the light breeze overhead. Far above, a red-tailed hawk circled, hunting for a small mammal to eat. We jogged down the river valley. A startled jackrabbit bounded away, its large, black-tipped ears visible above the tall grass. Sparrow Hawk wanted to race, so we ran until we reached a spring in a grove of oak and walnut trees. We drank and filled our pottery canteens before we took a path banked by wild grapes and thorny roses that led to the grassy **mesa.**

Soon we trotted through the knee-high grass dotted with juniper trees, scrub oaks, bear grass (the long, flexible leaves of which we weave into baskets), and yuccas. We dodged the long, sharp spines of the **prickly pear** and cholla cacti and the thorny **mesquite** bushes. My people harvest the fruit, flower, branches, and roots of these and many other plants. They give us medicine, arrow shafts, and many other things.

The wind pelted us with fine-grained desert sand, so we ran to an outcropping of honey-colored rock. Below the stones, out of the wind, we saw the deep holes gouged into the bedrock. People who harvest grass seeds and mesquite beans near here grind them into flour in these holes. This place is also a shrine, with sacred pictures engraved in the stone. My son and I stopped for a few minutes to pray and to leave an offering of cornmeal for our gods. Soon we were back on the mesa-top trail, running against the wind.

The sister village sits a short distance west of the Willow River. I saw Storyteller and his brother standing outside of the kiva. Storyteller is short, heavy, and clearly very strong. Although quiet, he's much respected. An attack by a **mountain lion** left him with scars and a limp. His real name is Turquoise Sky, but his friends call him "Storyteller" because he never gossips. Nearby, I noticed an older man softly singing as he wove at a blanket loom. My son saw someone else— Storyteller's young nephew Beaver—and shouted a welcome to his friend.

"Sparrow Hawk," Beaver called out. "I can come with you! My uncles say I can come with you to Chaco if your father approves. Will he?"

"Oh Beaver, he'll let you come, I know he will." Sparrow Hawk answered joyfully.

"Greetings, my good friend Storyteller," I said, smiling. "Who will ever talk to me again if I tell Beaver he can't come? Of course he'll come."

The boys ran off. Storyteller smiled at me, and we entered the kiva through a low passageway on the structure's easternmost side. I spotted a man working quietly at a loom and two strangers who I realized were the traders. Story-teller introduced me as his clan brother, and I learned that the men had come from a large town beyond Casas Grandes. We sat on mats near the hearth. Storyteller, the oldest of the four of us, led a brief prayer and passed a cloud-blower (pipe) around. Each of us blew the sacred smoke to the six directions. In the dim light, I saw bundles nearby, including three covered with blankets that seemed to be birdcages—with scarlet macaws inside.

They examined my goods while I looked through their large bags of shells. I picked out about two dozen large clamshells to use in mak-ing fine bracelets and pendants, two handfuls of the small shells that I could sew onto dance clothes, and a bunch of smooth, shining snail shells for necklaces.

Hours passed as we examined one another's goods. People wandered into the kiva to inspect the goods and to watch us trade, then left again as the day wore on. Finally, I agreed to trade what I had brought for the shells, 10 small copper bells, and one brilliantly colored scarlet macaw. Then they showed me something special—a hand-sized stone disc covered on one side by thinly sliced **pyrite** crystals. On the other side was a painted picture of a dancing man. I had heard of such things—mirrors—but had never seen one. The shiny surface reflected the firelight, and I could see my face in it. I knew that it would catch the rays of the sun and flash them around. The priests at Chaco would love it.

The traders wanted something special in exchange for the pyrite mirror. Reluctantly, I pulled a shell pendant out of a pouch I wore. I had gotten it years before in the land of the Hohokam. Tiny pieces of turquoise, pink shell, and lustrous abalone shells made a picture of a bird on the shell. For the pendant and two more bags of turquoise I would get the mirror. I'd leave the bags with White Bear for the traders to pick up in a few days.

Soon some women brought thick, tasty beans, meat stew, and freshly cooked piki bread. I had been too absorbed in the trading to notice that midday was long past. As we ate, the men described an exciting ball game and new rituals that they had seen in the south. I told them that the game sounded like one I saw the Hohokam play years ago. We agreed that traveling was never dull.

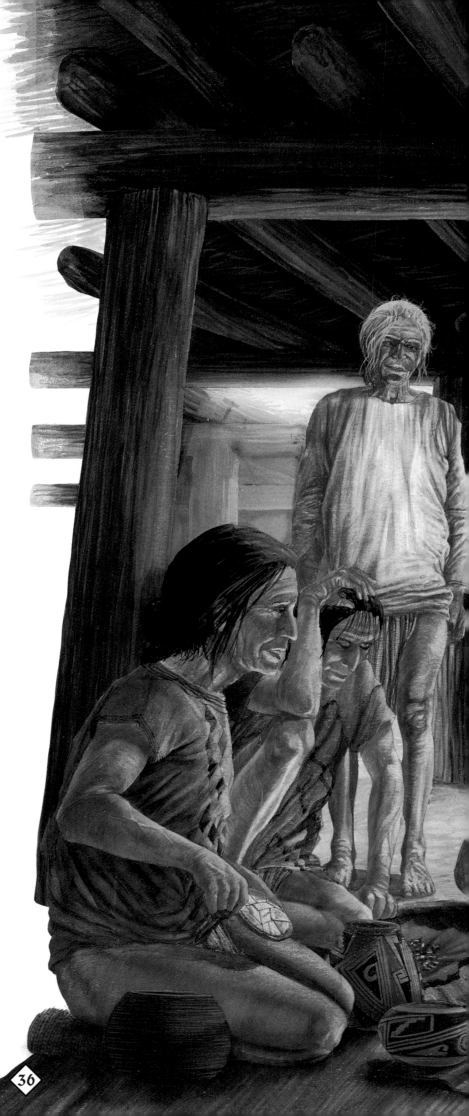

The sun was getting low in the sky, and we had to travel far the next day. It was time to go back to our village. Storyteller went to say his farewells, to get his cotton, and to collect the boys. My new friends, the traders, helped me pack. As a gift, they gave me two beautifully painted pots in colors that I had never seen before. I knew that White Shell would admire them.

A few hours of daylight were left when Storyteller and the boys returned. Our baskets were held to our backs by thick cotton cloth across our foreheads, and walking sticks helped us keep our balance. Storyteller's pack of personal supplies perched on his basket, and on mine sat the two gift pots. Beaver's extra blankets, sandals, and clothing were bundled on his back with the bag of shells. Sparrow Hawk carried the bird cage, and the mirror and bells were snug in a pouch that hung from my neck.

We were still 15 minutes from home when the sun set, lighting up the sky, the mountains, and our valley with brilliant colors. Rain that never reached the ground was falling from the dark clouds over the distant mountains, hinting at the rainy season that was still six weeks away. We were all silent as we walked, drinking in the colors and the sounds of the day's end. In my travels, I have never seen a place more beautiful than my homeland.

It was completely dark when we entered the village. We planned to spend the night in the kiva and to leave early the next morning, but first we walked to White Shell's house. The place was alive with people—our children, her family and mine, and our friends—waiting to bid us a safe journey. White Shell admired the new pots the traders had given me. I flashed the pyrite mirror in the firelight, and everyone urged me to keep it. I thought that I might, but I would show it to the priests at Chaco Canyon.

White Bear was there, sitting quietly. He and I had matters to discuss. We climbed the ladder to the roof, where I told him that I owed the traders from our sister village turquoise and that he should pay them in my absence. He reminded me to learn about new rituals performed by the priests at Chaco. The long drought and cold winters had made farming difficult everywhere, and the old rites didn't seem to be effective anymore.

By the time I had climbed back down into the house, most of the visitors were gone. I had wished friends good-bye while White Bear and I talked. I picked up Fawn, who was almost asleep on her feet, and promised to bring her presents from Chaco. I embraced White Shell and said my last farewells. Then, under a sky made bright by the Milky Way, I walked to the kiva and the start of a new adventure.

AFTERWORD

In the decades following Otherside's visit to Chaco Canyon, the changing climate, growing population, and periods of drought made it hard to live in the Mimbres River Valley. Within 50 years, the Mimbres moved toward the Rio Grande to build new towns. Over time, they probably became the Pueblo people known as the Zuni.

Explorers claimed the Pueblo's land for Spain in the 1500s and named the region New Mexico. Founded as the headquarters of New Mexico in 1609, Santa Fe drew Christian missionaries and soldiers. Missionaries forced the Pueblo to build and to attend Christian churches. Army officials made Native Americans lay roads, put up government buildings, produce trade goods, work as domestic slaves, and toil in mines and on farms.

In 1680 the Pueblo people overthrew the Spaniards, who re-captured the region in 1692. For the next 150 years, Spanish settlers and the Pueblo traded peacefully. The Pueblo absorbed elements of Spanish colonial culture, such as ranching. Fewer missionaries made their homes in the area, so Pueblo could practice their own religions.

New Mexico became part of the United States in 1848. Settlers from eastern U.S. states soon claimed much Pueblo territory. Throughout the twentieth century, the Pueblo people coped with the settlers and with U.S. government policies that fluctuated between appreciating Pueblo culture and trying to force **assimilation.** In 1910 and 1922, U.S. laws restored Native American land and paid for some land not returned. But in 1923, the U.S. government asked the Pueblo to abandon their religion. The government's return of nearly 50,000 acres of national forest in New Mexico was a Pueblo triumph in 1970.

The Pueblo still live in the Southwest. The tourist industry and outside jobs have replaced farms as the main suppliers of jobs and income. Most Pueblo homes have electricity, plumbing, and glass windows. Some Pueblo have moved far away to make more money. Despite these changes, Pueblo people still preserve traditions that may date all the way back to the Mimbres.

GLOSSARY

adobe: A type of clay soil found in Mexico and in dry parts of the United States that can be shaped into bricks.

animism: A belief system in which every object is believed to be alive.

archaeologist: A scientist who studies the material remains of past human life.

artifact: An item crafted by a human.

assimiliation: The process of one culture absorbing the beliefs and lifestyle of another. For example, the U.S. government tried to force Native Americans to discard their own culture and replace it with mainstream U.S. culture.

ball game: A Native American game that involved kicking a wooden or rubber ball. Ball games often pitted communities against one another.

cholla: A large cactus also called "walking stick." It has sharp spines, beautiful flowers and edible fruit.

cotton: Fluffy fibers surrounding cottonseeds. The seeds were eaten, and the fibers could be woven into strong, lightweight, and flexible fabrics.

draft animal: A tame animal that humans use to pull carts.

Horn Mountain: A fictional name for the distinctive mountain peak known as Cookes Peak. It is in the part of the Mogollon Mountain range known as the Mimbres Mountains.

kiva: A ceremonial room used by modern Pueblo Indian people. Kivas were used throughout the Southwest but differed in appearance.

mesa: A broad, flat area of land that rises up from lower land, usually with steep sides.

mesquite: A bush with long thorns and nutritious pods that were ground into flour.

mountain lion: A large cat native to North America, also called puma, cougar, or panther.

northern mountains: The Mogollon Mountains. Named for an eighteenth-century governor of New Mexico, these slopes are also called the Gilas. The Mogollon culture was named after this mountain range.

piki: Thin cornmeal bread cooked on a hot stone.

piñon: A small pine tree whose nutritious nuts were important parts of the ancient Puebloan diet.

plaza: An open area, often paved with large stones and surrounded by buildings. These communal areas served as dining rooms, work rooms, and meeting places for the ancient Mimbres and other southwestern people.

prickly pear: A cactus with large, round leaves (pads) and red fruit.

pueblo: Spanish-speaking settlers applied this word, meaning "town" in Spanish, to the villages of the Southwest. These days the Native Americans of the Southwest are sometimes referred to as Pueblo Indians.

purification ritual: A religious rite to purge the spirit of undesirable elements. Some Native American cultures consider dangerous activities like warfare, hunting large animals, and traveling to be bad for the spirit. Purification rituals set things right again.

pyrite: Known as "fool's gold" because of its golden color, pyrite is a common iron ore often found in the form of crystals.

ramada: The Spanish word for a kind of sunshade or shelter. Mimbres ramadas had roofs, but no sides, and projected from the side of a house.

solstice: The time of the year when the sun reaches either the point farthest north of the equator or the point farthest south of the equator. These longest (or shortest) days of the year are often marked by ceremonies. The Mimbres may have kept a yearly calendar by observing the sun, moon, and stars.

Southwest: The arid region in the southwestern corner of the United States, encompassing the states of New Mexico and Arizona. The deserts of northernmost Mexico are part of the same climate zone.

sun priest: An important religious leader who was responsible for keeping a calendar so that rituals could be held and fields planted at the proper time.

terrace: An area of high, flat land on each side of a waterway.

turkey-feather blanket: A warm, durable cover made by southwestern people. They first twisted turkey feathers with yucca-fiber cords that were then woven into soft, warm blankets.

turkey vulture: Also called a buzzard, a large, broad-winged bird of prey that usually feeds on carrion (rotten and raw meat).

yucca: A tall plant with long, stiff leaves and white flowers. Banana yucca and soaptree yucca thrived in Mimbres country. Their spiky leaves grow in mounds, and they have large central flower stalks. The leaves were processed into rope, fiber, and paint brushes. The flowers and fruit were eaten and used as medicine. The roots were made into soap.

PRONUNCIATION GUIDE

adobe	ah-DOH-bee
Casas Grandes	CAH-sahs GRAHN-days
cholla	CHOY-yah
kiva	KEE-vah
mesa	MAY-sah
Mimbres	MIM-bress
piki	PEE-kee
piñon	PIH-nyon
pueblo	PWEH-bloh
ramada	rah MAH dah
yucca	YUH-kah

FURTHER READING

Cory, Stephen. *Pueblo Indian.* Minneapolis: Lerner Publications Company, 1996.

Early, Theresa S. *New Mexico.* Minneapolis: Lerner Publications Company, 1993.

Naranjo, Tito. *A Day With a Pueblo.* Minneapolis: Runestone Press, 1999.

Ortiz, Alfonzo. *The Pueblo.* New York: Chelsea House Publishers, 1994.

Rina, Swentzell. *Children of Clay: A Family of Pueblo Potters.* Minneapolis: Lerner Publications Company, 1992.

Young, Robert. *A Personal Tour of Mesa Verde.* Minneapolis: Lerner Publications Company, 1999.

INDEX

ABOUT THE
AUTHOR AND THE ILLUSTRATOR

J. J. Brody is a professor emeritus of art and art history at the University of New Mexico, Albuquerque, and former director of the Maxwell Museum of Anthropology in Albuquerque. He is a research associate at the School of American Research and at the Laboratory of Anthropology and Museum of Indian Art and Culture in Santa Fe, New Mexico. A graduate in art of the Cooper Union, Dr. Brody earned a doctorate in art history at the University of New Mexico. His research area is the prehistoric and historic American Indian art of the Southwest. His previous books include *Indian Painters and White Patrons*, *Mimbres Painted Pottery*, *The Anasazi*, and *Anasazi and Pueblo Painting*.

Giorgio Bacchin, a native of Milan, Italy, studied the graphic arts in his hometown. After years of freelance graphic design, Mr. Bacchin has completely devoted himself to book illustration. His works have appeared in educational and trade publications.